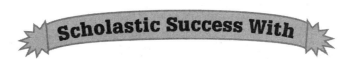

Scholastic Success With

CHARTS, TABLES & GRAPHS

GRADES 3–4

by

Michael Priestley

D1613817

SCHOLASTIC
PROFESSIONAL BOOKS

NEW YORK • TORONTO • LONDON • AUCKLAND • SYDNEY
MEXICO CITY • NEW DELHI • HONG KONG • BUENOS AIRES

Cover design by Maria Lilja
Interior design by Solutions by Design, Inc.
Interior illustrations by James Graham Hale

ISBN: 0-439-29706-0

2 3 4 5 6 7 8 9 10   40   08 07 06 05 04 03

TABLE OF CONTENTS

Introduction to Teachers

Tables, charts, and graphs are essential visual aids for helping students comprehend and analyze information in many different subjects. In early grades, instruction generally focuses on helping students read and understand the information presented. In later grades, students must also be able to analyze the data, draw conclusions and make predictions based on the data, and evaluate information in different sources and different formats.

This book will help your students practice using these visual aids. As your students solve the problems, they'll develop skills in reading and interpreting information. They'll also discover how much fun learning to use tables, charts, and graphs can be!

HOW TO USE THIS BOOK

The purpose of this book is to provide interesting and challenging graphic aids for practice and instruction. They can also be used to help prepare students for standardized tests that include these kinds of materials.

The subject-area content and the types of charts, tables, and graphs presented in this book are based on the material students will encounter in major standardized tests, including the Stanford Achievement Test, CTBS TerraNova, Metropolitan Achievement Test, Iowa Test of Basic Skills, and the California Achievement Test. State-wide assessments and state curriculum standards have also been used to help determine the content and skills covered in this book.

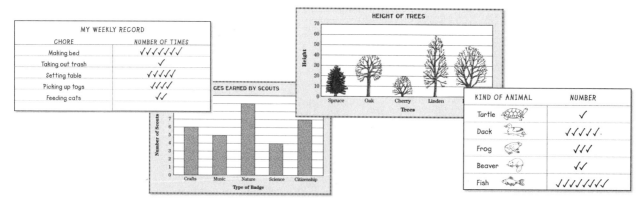

This book provides 43 pages of graphic aids with the following features:

- High-interest topics and up-to-date information

- Grade-appropriate tables, charts, and graphs

- Material organized by subject area and keyed to the curricula in Mathematics, Reading/Language Arts, Social Studies, and Science

- Pages structured as workbook activities for student practice and instruction

- A set of 4–8 questions accompanying each graphic that resemble the kinds of questions students will see on standardized tests

The questions with these activities are designed to measure critical thinking skills, such as interpreting and analyzing data, summarizing information, drawing conclusions, and evaluating information. These questions will help you assess students' understanding of the material and will help students practice answering test questions. Depending on the activity, questions include multiple-choice items, short-answer items, and/or written response items that require longer answers. Some pages require students to construct tables or graphs from given information. Answers to the questions may be found in the Answer Key beginning on page 45.

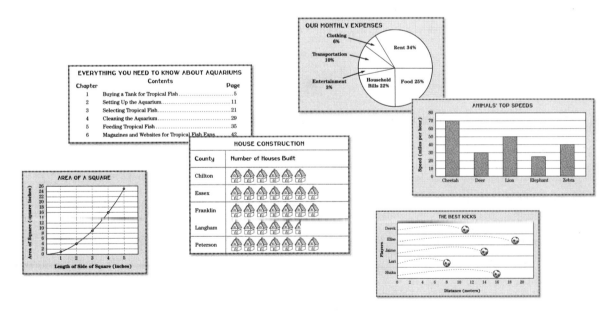

Name _____   Date _____

The Winning Team

This table displays the win-loss record for five major-league baseball teams in 2000. Use the table to choose the best answer to each question below.

BASEBALL STANDINGS: AMERICAN LEAGUE EAST

Team	Wins	Losses	Percent	Games Behind
New York Yankees	87	74	.540	—
Boston Red Sox	85	77	.525	$2\frac{1}{2}$
Toronto Blue Jays	83	79	.512	$4\frac{1}{2}$
Baltimore Orioles	74	88	.457	$13\frac{1}{2}$
Tampa Bay Devil Rays	69	92	.429	18

1 Which team had the most wins?
  ⓐ Baltimore Orioles   ⓒ New York Yankees
  ⓑ Boston Red Sox   ⓓ Toronto Blue Jays

2 How many games did the Boston Red Sox lose?
  ⓐ 74   ⓒ 79
  ⓑ 77   ⓓ 85

3 Which team had 74 wins and 88 losses?
  ⓐ New York Yankees   ⓒ Toronto Blue Jays
  ⓑ Boston Red Sox   ⓓ Baltimore Orioles

4 How many games did the Tampa Bay Devil Rays win?
  ⓐ 69   ⓒ 83
  ⓑ 74   ⓓ 92

5 How many of these teams won more than half of their games?
  ⓐ 2   ⓒ 4
  ⓑ 3   ⓓ 5

Scholastic Success With Charts, Tables & Graphs: Grades 3–4 ● Scholastic Professional Books

Name _____ Date _____

Measuring Up

Mrs. Umberto made this table to use when she buys clothing for her children. Use the table to answer the questions below.

MY CHILDREN'S CLOTHING SIZES			
Child	Height (inches)	Weight (pounds)	Size
Emilio	60	103	14
Teresita	54	75	12
Pablo	52	60	8
Juana	43	51	5

1 How tall is Emilio? _____

2 How much more does Teresita weigh than Juana?

_____

3 Which two children are about the same height?

_____

4 What size clothing does Juana wear?

_____

5 According to this table, how do children's clothing sizes change as children grow taller?

_____

Name _____   Date _____

Tori's Sandwich Study

Tori asked her classmates to name their favorite sandwiches. She made a tally chart showing how many kids chose each kind. Use the chart to choose the best answer to each question below.

OUR FAVORITE SANDWICHES	
KIND OF SANDWICH	NUMBER OF KIDS
Ham and cheese	✓✓✓✓
Tuna fish	✓✓✓
Peanut butter and jelly	✓✓✓✓✓
Egg salad	✓✓

1 How many kids named tuna fish as their favorite kind of sandwich?

    ⓐ 2   ⓒ 4

    ⓑ 3   ⓓ 5

2 How many kids named egg salad?

    ⓐ 2   ⓒ 4

    ⓑ 3   ⓓ 5

3 Which kind of sandwich was named by the most kids?

    ⓐ ham and cheese   ⓒ peanut butter and jelly

    ⓑ tuna fish   ⓓ egg salad

4 If each kid named only one favorite sandwich, how many kids in all answered Tori's question?

    ⓐ 4   ⓒ 12

    ⓑ 5   ⓓ 14

Name _____ Date _____

Pete's Chores

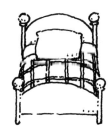

Pete made this tally chart to show how often he did chores around the house. He recorded his chores for one week. Use the chart to choose the best answer to each question below.

MY WEEKLY RECORD	
CHORE	NUMBER OF TIMES
Making bed	✓✓✓✓✓✓
Taking out trash	✓
Setting table	✓✓✓✓✓
Picking up toys	✓✓✓✓
Feeding cats	✓✓✓

1 Which chore did Pete do most often?
- (a) making bed
- (b) setting table
- (c) picking up toys
- (d) feeding cats

2 How many times did Pete take out the trash?
- (a) 5
- (b) 4
- (c) 3
- (d) 1

3 How many times did Pete set the table?
- (a) 4
- (b) 5
- (c) 6
- (d) 7

4 How many times in all did Pete do chores?
- (a) 13
- (b) 14
- (c) 17
- (d) 20

Name _____ Date _____

Drew's Newspaper Route

Drew made a pictograph to show how many newspapers he delivers on each street of his newspaper route. Use the graph to choose the best answer to each question below.

MY DAILY DELIVERIES

Gold Street	🗞🗞🗞🗞🗞🗞🗞
Harold Street	🗞🗞🗞🗞🗞🗞🗞🗞🗞🗞
Lower Road	🗞🗞🗞
Morris Drive	🗞🗞🗞🗞🗞🗞
Burnham Street	🗞🗞🗞🗞🗞🗞🗞🗞

Each 🗞 stands for one newspaper.

1 How many newspapers does Drew deliver on Morris Drive?
- ⓐ 6
- ⓑ 7
- ⓒ 8
- ⓓ 9

2 On which street does Drew deliver the most newspapers?
- ⓐ Harold Street
- ⓑ Gold Street
- ⓒ Morris Drive
- ⓓ Lower Road

3 How many more newspapers does Drew deliver on Burnham Street than on Lower Road?
- ⓐ 7
- ⓑ 5
- ⓒ 3
- ⓓ 1

4 What is the total number of newspapers Drew delivers on his newspaper route?
- ⓐ 38
- ⓑ 36
- ⓒ 33
- ⓓ 30

Name _____ Date _____

Cool Inventions

Third graders in the Town School asked all the students to name the most important invention of the last 200 years. This pictograph shows how many students chose each of the inventions listed. Use the graph to answer the questions below.

KIDS' CHOICES	
Automobile	🚶 🚶 🚶 🚶
Computer	🚶 🚶 🚶 🚶 🚶 🚶 🚶
Electric light	🚶 🚶 🚶
Telephone	🚶 🚶 🚶 🚶
Television	🚶 🚶 🚶 🚶 🚶 🚶

KEY
🚶 = 5 students

1 Which invention was named by the most students?

_____

2 How many students named television as the most important invention?

_____

3 Which two inventions were named by an equal number of students?

_____

4 How many more students named the computer than the electric light?

_____

Name _____   Date _____

The Class Field Trip

Mrs. Smith's class took a field trip to the park, and a park ranger explained how different trees grow to different heights. This bar graph shows the trees' heights. Use the graph to choose the best answer to each question below.

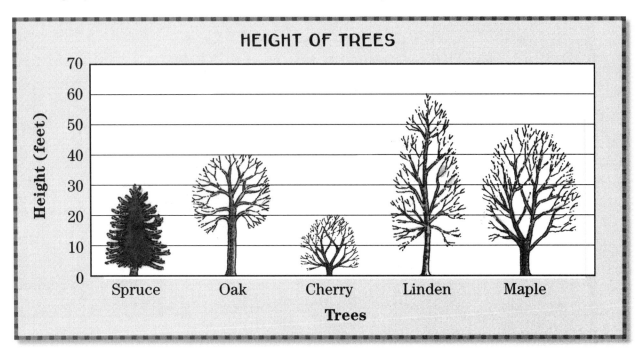

1 Which tree is the shortest?

   ⓐ cherry   ⓒ maple

   ⓑ linden   ⓓ spruce

2 How tall is the oak tree?

   ⓐ 20 feet   ⓒ 40 feet

   ⓑ 30 feet   ⓓ 50 feet

3 Which tree is twice as tall as the spruce?

   ⓐ maple   ⓒ cherry

   ⓑ linden   ⓓ oak

4 How much taller is the maple tree than the cherry tree?

   ⓐ 40 feet   ⓒ 20 feet

   ⓑ 30 feet   ⓓ 10 feet

Name _____ Date _____

Hannah and Her Cousins

Hannah's cousins live in five different states. She made this bar graph to show how many cousins live in each state. Use the graph to answer the questions below.

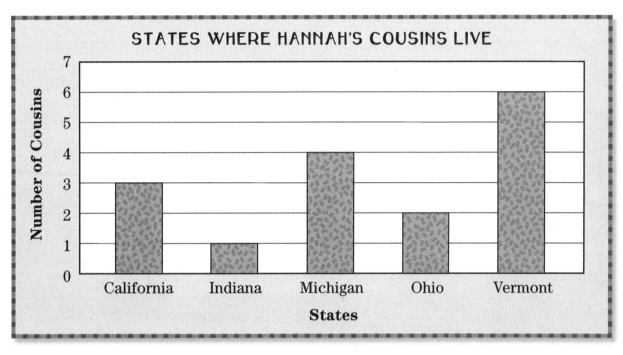

1 How many cousins live in Ohio?

_____

2 The greatest number of Hannah's cousins live in which state?

_____

3 How many more cousins live in Michigan than in California?

_____

4 How many cousins does Hannah have altogether?

_____

Name _____   Date _____

Soccer Contest

Five friends held a contest to see how far they could kick a soccer ball. The bar graph below shows the results of their contest. Use the graph to choose the best answer to each question.

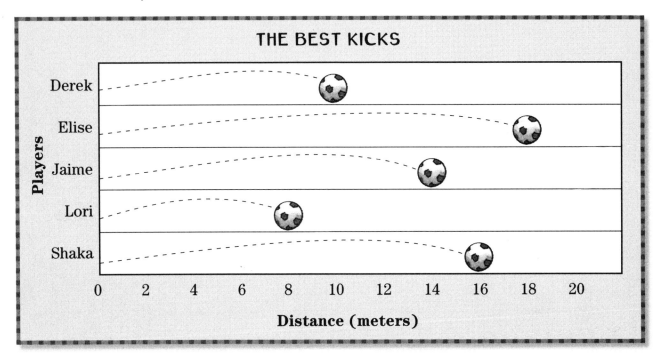

THE BEST KICKS

1 Who won the contest?
- ⓐ Derek
- ⓑ Elise
- ⓒ Lori
- ⓓ Shaka

2 How far did Jaime kick the ball?
- ⓐ 8 meters
- ⓑ 10 meters
- ⓒ 12 meters
- ⓓ 14 meters

3 Who kicked the ball half as far as Shaka?
- ⓐ Elise
- ⓑ Lori
- ⓒ Jaime
- ⓓ Derek

4 Compared with Derek, how much farther did Elise kick the ball?
- ⓐ 12 meters
- ⓑ 10 meters
- ⓒ 8 meters
- ⓓ 6 meters

Name _____ Date _____

Scouts' Honors

The Adventure Scouts earn badges by doing special projects. Their scout leader made this bar graph to show how many scouts have earned each type of badge. Use the graph to answer the questions below.

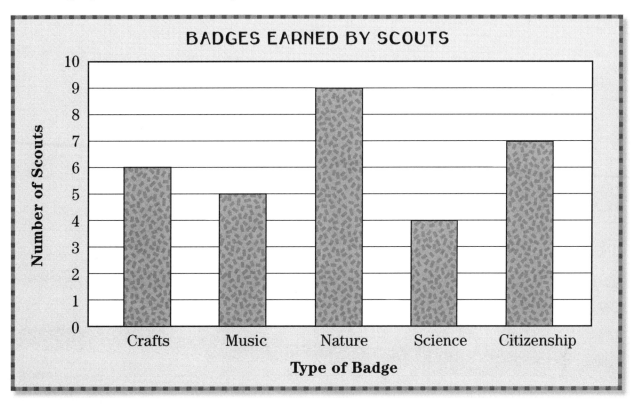

1 How many scouts have earned a music badge? _____

2 How many more scouts have earned citizenship badges than science badges?

_____

3 Which badge has been earned by the most scouts?

_____

4 How many badges have been earned altogether? _____

5 Which type of badge is most difficult to earn? Explain your thinking below.

_____

_____

Name _____   Date _____

Zack's Lazy Afternoon

Zack spent an afternoon at Sunrise Pond. He made this tally chart to show how many animals he saw at the pond.

KIND OF ANIMAL	NUMBER
Turtle	✓
Duck	✓✓✓✓✓
Frog	✓✓✓
Beaver	✓✓
Fish	✓✓✓✓✓✓

Then Zack started making a bar graph of the animals he saw at the pond, but didn't have time to finish it. Use the tally chart to finish Zack's bar graph.

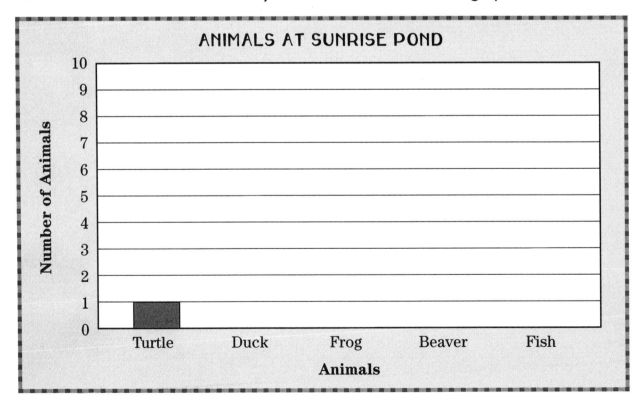

ANIMALS AT SUNRISE POND

16

Name _____ Date _____

The Class Takes a Trip

Mrs. Fieldstone's students live in Boston, Massachusetts. They took a vote to decide where to go for their class trip in May and made a circle graph to help analyze the results. Use the graph to answer the questions.

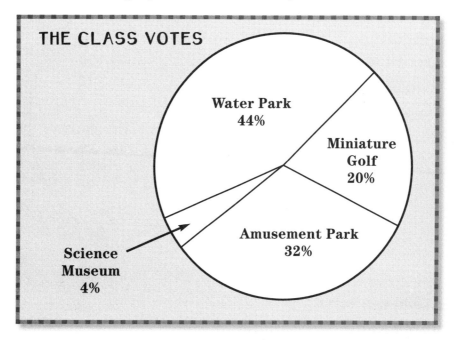

THE CLASS VOTES

Water Park 44%

Miniature Golf 20%

Amusement Park 32%

Science Museum 4%

1 Which choice received the fewest votes?

_____

2 If there are 25 students in the class, how many voted for miniature golf?

_____

3 Which two activities together were picked by about $\frac{3}{4}$ of the students?

_____

4 Which activity was chosen by about $\frac{1}{3}$ of the students?

_____

5 How do you think the votes would be different if the class trip took place in February instead of May?

_____

_____

Name _____ Date _____

Recycling Efforts

Every week, the town of Galway collects trash for recycling. The circle graph on the right shows what kinds of items are collected. Use the graph to choose the best answer to each question below.

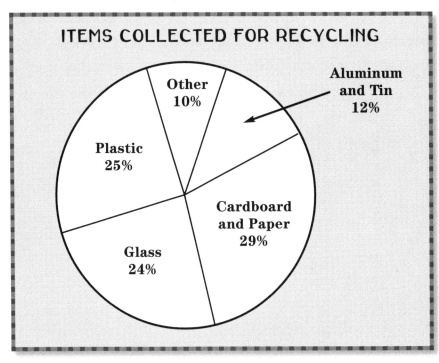

ITEMS COLLECTED FOR RECYCLING

Other 10%
Aluminum and Tin 12%
Plastic 25%
Cardboard and Paper 29%
Glass 24%

1 Cardboard and paper make up what percentage of the recycled items?
   (a) 12%   (c) 25%
   (b) 24%   (d) 29%

2 What fraction shows what part of the recycled items are plastic?
   (a) $\frac{1}{4}$ (c) $\frac{1}{2}$
   (b) $\frac{1}{3}$ (d) $\frac{2}{3}$

3 Of every 100 items recycled, how many are glass?
   (a) 10   (c) 15
   (b) 12   (d) 24

4 What percentage of the recycled items are aluminum and tin?
   (a) 10%   (c) 24%
   (b) 12%   (d) 25%

5 One half of the items in the "Other" category were batteries. If batteries were shown on the graph, what percentage would they represent?
   (a) 50%   (c) 5%
   (b) 10%   (d) 3%

Name _____ Date _____

Best-Selling Books

The line graph below shows how many books were sold each day at a school book fair. Use the graph to answer the questions.

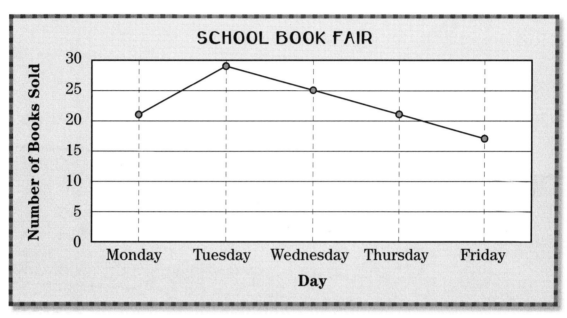

1 How many books were sold on Monday? _____

2 On what day were the same number of books sold as on Monday?

_____

3 How many more books were sold on Tuesday than on Thursday?

_____

4 What was the greatest number of books sold in one day?

_____

5 If the sales trend continued to Saturday, how many books would you expect to sell on Saturday?

_____

Name _____ Date _____

Compare the Squares

The line graph below shows the areas of squares of different sizes. Use the graph to answer the questions.

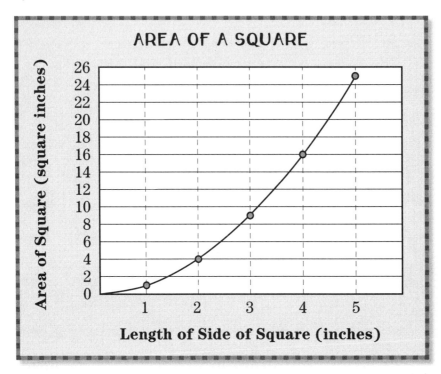

1 What is the area of a square with sides that are 4 inches long?

_____

2 If the area of a square is 25 square inches, how long are its sides?

_____

3 What is the approximate area of a square with 4.5-inch sides?

_____

4 About how long are the sides of a square with an area of 12 square inches?

_____

5 Write one or two sentences describing the trend shown on this line graph.

_____

_____

Scholastic Success With Charts, Tables & Graphs: Grades 3–4 ● Scholastic Professional Books

Name _____ Date _____

Adorable Animals

Do you know what a baby goat is called? The chart below provides the names for many baby animals. Use the chart to choose the best answer to each question.

NAMES FOR BABY ANIMALS			
Animal	Name for Baby	Animal	Name for Baby
Bear	Cub	Fox	Kit
Cow	Calf	Goat	Kid
Deer	Fawn	Kangaroo	Joey
Dog	Pup	Sheep	Lamb

1 What is the name for a baby deer?
    (a) cub   (c) fawn
    (b) calf   (d) pup

2 What is a baby fox called?
    (a) kit   (c) cub
    (b) kid   (d) lamb

3 Which kind of animal has cubs?
    (a) goat   (c) kangaroo
    (b) sheep   (d) bear

4 A "joey" is what kind of animal?
    (a) cow   (c) kangaroo
    (b) fox   (d) sheep

5 A baby goat is a —
    (a) kid   (c) pup
    (b) lamb   (d) calf

Name _____ Date _____

Joel's Trip Planner

Joel made a chart for his family to help them plan trips to local parks. Use the chart to answer the questions below.

THINGS TO DO AT LOCAL PARKS	
Blue Summit Park	🚶 ⛱ ⛺
Lilac Lake Park	⛱ 🏊
Mead Canyon Park	🚶 ⛱ 🏊 ⛺
Pinetop Park	⛱ ⛺
Underwood Park	🚶 ⛺

KEY

🚶 **Hiking Trails**

⛱ **Picnic Area**

🏊 **Swimming Beach**

⛺ **Campground**

1 What can visitors do at Underwood Park?

_____

2 How many parks have a picnic area? _____

3 Which parks have a swimming beach?

_____

4 Which park offers the most activities?

_____

5 In which park can you ONLY camp or hike?

_____

Scholastic Success With Charts, Tables & Graphs: Grades 3–4 ● Scholastic Professional Books

Name _____ Date _____

Ordering Dinner

The Magic Meal Restaurant has a special children's menu. Use the chart to choose the best answer to each question below.

CHILDREN'S MENU

Sandwiches   *Served with potato chips and a pickle*

Egg Salad $2.50
Ham Salad $3.00
Tuna Fish $2.75
Grilled Cheese $2.50

Dinners   *Served with salad and a dinner roll*

Macaroni and Cheese $3.75
Spaghetti $3.00
Chicken Pot Pie $4.00
Beef Stew $4.00

Drinks

Milk, Chocolate Milk, Lemonade $1.00

Desserts

Dish of Ice Cream or Pudding $1.50

---

1 How much does a grilled cheese sandwich cost?

(a) $2.50   (c) $3.00
(b) $2.75   (d) $3.50

2 Which food is served with any dinner on the menu?

(a) ice cream   (c) salad
(b) potato chips   (d) pudding

3 Which drink is listed on the menu?

(a) milk shake   (c) orange juice
(b) lemonade   (d) hot chocolate

4 How much does a spaghetti dinner cost?

(a) $4.00   (c) $3.00
(b) $3.75   (d) $2.50

Name _____ Date _____

The Bookworm Club

Use this chart from the Bookworm Club to answer the questions below.

OUR BOOKS OF THE MONTH		
Item Number	Title	Price
1	*Amy Grows Up*	$3.25
2	*Beginner's Luck*	$2.95
3	*Dinosaur Dig*	$4.50
4	*Famous Firsts*	$3.95
5	*Jump Rope Games*	$4.25
6	*Lightning and Thunder*	$2.95
7	*Never Say Never*	$3.50
8	*Queen Mary of Scotland*	$2.95
9	*Science in Your Kitchen*	$3.25
10	*Yellowstone Park*	$4.50

1 What is the title of item number **1** on the book list?

_____

2 How much does the book *Queen Mary of Scotland* cost?

_____

3 What is the item number of the book *Jump Rope Games*?

_____

4 Look at this part of a book order form. Fill in the missing information.

Item Number	Title	Price
3		

Name _____ Date _____

Niko's Aquarium

Niko wants to set up an aquarium for tropical fish. He is reading a library book about aquariums before he begins this project. Use the table to choose the best answer to each question below.

TROPICAL FISH AQUARIUMS
Contents

Chapter		Page
1	Buying a Tank for Tropical Fish............................5	
2	Setting up the Aquarium....................................11	
3	Selecting Tropical Fish.....................................21	
4	Cleaning the Aquarium.....................................29	
5	Feeding Tropical Fish 35	
6	Magazines and Websites for Tropical Fish Fans........42	

1 Niko wonders which fish get along well in an aquarium. Which chapter should he read to find this information?

    ⓐ chapter 1   ⓒ chapter 5

    ⓑ chapter 3   ⓓ chapter 6

2 Which of Niko's questions about tropical fish aquariums is probably answered in Chapter 2?

    ⓐ How much gravel should I put in the bottom of the tank?

    ⓑ How often should I feed my fish?

    ⓒ How can I be sure I'm buying healthy fish?

    ⓓ How much will a five-gallon tank cost?

3 Where should Niko start reading to find out how to clean the sides of his aquarium?

    ⓐ page 5   ⓒ page 21

    ⓑ page 11   ⓓ page 29

4 Which chapter explains how to find information about tropical fish online?

    ⓐ chapter 2   ⓒ chapter 5

    ⓑ chapter 4   ⓓ chapter 6

Name _____ Date _____

Card Sharks

Do you like to play cards? Use the table to choose the best answer to each question below.

LET'S PLAY CARDS
Contents

1 Which chapter has information about games for two players?
  (a) chapter 1   (c) chapter 3
  (b) chapter 2   (d) chapter 4

2 Where should you start reading if you need to find out what a "wild card" is?
  (a) page 7   (c) page 21
  (b) page 12   (d) page 24

3 Which game might be a good one to play with three friends?
  (a) Beehive   (c) Hit or Miss
  (b) Jacks   (d) Gops

4 The directions for playing Spade Oklahoma begin on which page?
  (a) page 14   (c) page 17
  (b) page 15   (d) page 19

Name _____ Date _____

School Birthdays

The table below shows how many students in Grades 3 and 4 at the Rand School were born during each month. Use the table to answer the questions.

BIRTHDAY UPDATE												
Month of Birth	Sep.	Oct.	Nov.	Dec.	Jan.	Feb.	Mar.	Apr.	May	June	July	Aug.
Number of Students	2	1	2	3	2	4	6	9	6	5	4	3
Season	Fall			Winter			Spring			Summer		

1 How many students were born in November? _____

2 What month had the same number of births as February?

_____

3 How many students were born in the fall?

_____

4 During which season were the most students born?

_____

5 In which month would it be most likely to have two students share the same birthday?

_____

Name _____ Date _____

Presidential Studies

The table below shows information about recent presidents of the United States. Use the table to choose the best answer to each question.

U.S. PRESIDENTS SINCE 1970			
Number	Name	Birth–Death	Years in Office
37	Richard M. Nixon	1913–1994	1969–1974
38	Gerald R. Ford	1913–	1974–1977
39	Jimmy Carter	1924–	1977–1981
40	Ronald Reagan	1911–	1981–1989
41	George Bush	1924–	1989–1993
42	William J. Clinton	1946–	1993–2001
43	George W. Bush	1946–	2001–

1 Who was the 40th president of the United States?
- (a) Gerald Ford
- (b) Jimmy Carter
- (c) Ronald Reagan
- (d) George Bush

2 In what year was Richard Nixon born?
- (a) 1911
- (b) 1913
- (c) 1924
- (d) 1946

3 Which president spent the shortest time in office?
- (a) Richard Nixon
- (b) George Bush
- (c) Jimmy Carter
- (d) Gerald Ford

4 Who was president in 1992?
- (a) Jimmy Carter
- (b) Ronald Reagan
- (c) George Bush
- (d) Bill Clinton

5 Which number president is George W. Bush?
- (a) 43
- (b) 42
- (c) 41
- (d) 40

Name _____ Date _____

Beautiful Bridges

The chart below lists six of the longest suspension bridges
in the United States. Use the chart to answer the questions.

SUSPENSION BRIDGES OF THE UNITED STATES			
Year Completed	Bridge	Location	Main Span (feet)
1931	George Washington	New York–New Jersey	3,500
1937	Golden Gate	California	4,200
1950	Tacoma Narrows	Washington	2,800
1957	Mackinac Straits	Michigan	3,800
1964	Verrazano–Narrows	New York	4,260
1968	Delaware Memorial	Delaware	2,150

1 Which bridge has the longest main span?

_____

2 Which bridge was completed in 1957, and where is it located?

_____

3 Where is the Golden Gate Bridge, and when was it completed?

_____

4 How long is the main span of the George Washington Bridge?

_____

5 If the chart listed these bridges from shortest to longest, which two bridges
would be listed first?

_____

Name _____ Date _____

The Wild Wild West

The chart below provides information about six states in the western United States. Use the chart to answer the questions.

WESTERN STATES				
State	Capital	Date of Statehood	State Bird	State Flower
Colorado	Denver	1876	Lark Bunting	Rocky Mountain Columbine
Idaho	Boise	1890	Mountain Bluebird	Syringa
Nevada	Carson City	1864	Mountain Bluebird	Sagebrush
Oregon	Salem	1859	Western Meadowlark	Oregon Grape
Utah	Salt Lake City	1896	Seagull	Sego Lily
Washington	Olympia	1889	Willow Goldfinch	Western Rhododendron

1 What is the capital of Washington? _____

2 In what year did Idaho become a state? _____

3 Which of these states gained statehood first? _____

4 What is Colorado's state bird? _____

5 Salem is the capital of which state? _____

6 What is Nevada's state flower? _____

7 Which states have the same state bird, and what bird is it?

_____

Name _____ Date _____

The Story of Paper

The flow chart below shows how paper is made. Use the chart to answer the
questions.

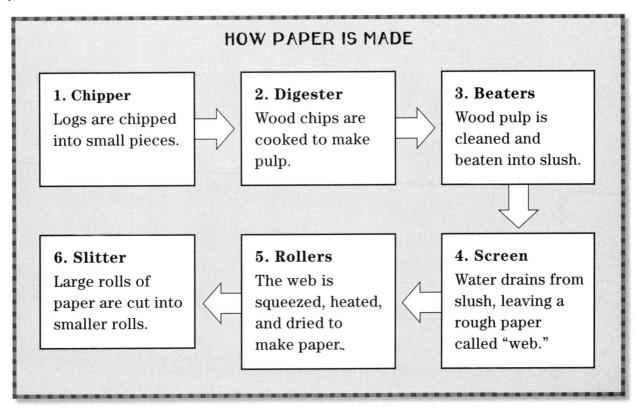

HOW PAPER IS MADE

1. Chipper
Logs are chipped
into small pieces.

2. Digester
Wood chips are
cooked to make
pulp.

3. Beaters
Wood pulp is
cleaned and
beaten into slush.

6. Slitter
Large rolls of
paper are cut into
smaller rolls.

5. Rollers
The web is
squeezed, heated,
and dried to
make paper.

4. Screen
Water drains from
slush, leaving a
rough paper
called "web."

1 What is the first step in making paper?

_____

2 What happens in the "beaters"?

_____

3 In which step does slush become rough paper?

_____

4 What tasks are done with the use of heat?

_____

_____

Name _____ Date _____

Building Houses

The pictograph below shows the number of new houses built in five different counties last year. Use the graph to answer the questions.

HOUSE CONSTRUCTION	
County	Number of Houses Built
Chilton	🏠🏠🏠🏠🏠🏠
Essex	🏠🏠🏠🏠🏠🏠🏠🏠
Franklin	🏠🏠🏠🏠🏠🏠🏠🏠🏠
Langham	🏠🏠🏠🏠🏠
Peterson	🏠🏠🏠🏠🏠🏠🏠🏠

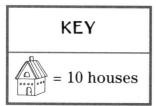

KEY

🏠 = 10 houses

1 How many houses were built in Chilton County last year?

_____

2 In which county were the most houses built?

_____

3 In which county were the fewest houses built?

_____

4 How many more houses were built in Peterson County than in Langham County?

_____

5 A total of 42 houses were built in Winwood County last year. How would this number be shown on the graph? (Draw a picture on the back of this paper.)

Scholastic Success With Charts, Tables & Graphs: Grades 3–4 ● Scholastic Professional Books

Name _____ Date _____

How Does Susan's Garden Grow?

Susan made a bar graph showing the heights of the flowers in her garden. Use the graph to choose the best answers to the questions below.

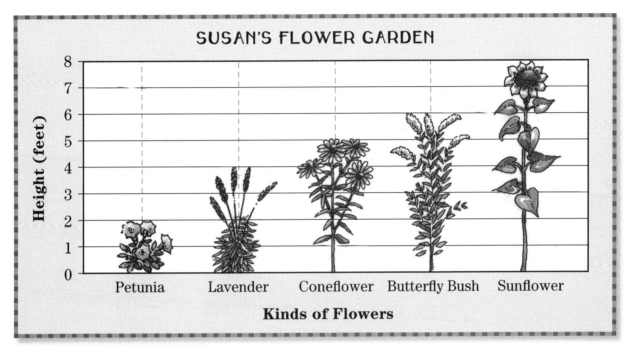

1 How tall is the coneflower?
   ⓐ 3 feet
   ⓑ 4 feet
   ⓒ 5 feet
   ⓓ 6 feet

2 Which plant is tallest?
   ⓐ lavender
   ⓑ coneflower
   ⓒ butterfly bush
   ⓓ sunflower

3 Which plant is 4 feet tall?
   ⓐ petunia
   ⓑ lavender
   ⓒ coneflower
   ⓓ butterfly bush

4 Which plant is three times as tall as the petunia?
   ⓐ lavender
   ⓑ coneflower
   ⓒ butterfly bush
   ⓓ sunflower

5 Which plant is closest in height to the lavender?
   ⓐ petunia
   ⓑ coneflower
   ⓒ butterfly bush
   ⓓ sunflower

Name _____   Date _____

Alex the Sports Reporter

Alex conducted a survey of his classmates about their favorite team and individual sports. He made these charts to show the results of his survey. Use the charts to make your own bar graphs.

FAVORITE TEAM SPORTS	
Basketball	HHT HHT III
Soccer	HHT HHT II
Hockey	HHT III
Softball	HHT I

FAVORITE INDIVIDUAL SPORTS	
Tennis	HHT HHT III
Running	HHT
Golf	HHT I
Swimming	HHT HHT HHT

1. On the grid below, make a bar graph to show how many students picked each *team* sport. Be sure to include labels and a title.

2. On the grid below, make a bar graph to show how many students picked each *individual* sport. Be sure to include labels and a title.

Name _____ Date _____

Mindy Minds the Money

Mindy and her Dad made a circle graph to show how the family's money was spent each month. Use the graph to choose the best answer to each question below.

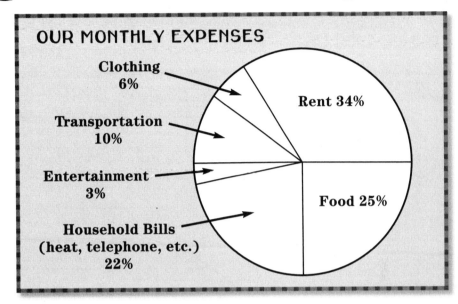

OUR MONTHLY EXPENSES

Clothing 6%
Rent 34%
Transportation 10%
Entertainment 3%
Food 25%
Household Bills (heat, telephone, etc.) 22%

1 Which is the largest cost each month?
ⓐ food
ⓑ rent
ⓒ clothing
ⓓ transportation

2 How much of the money spent each month goes to food?
ⓐ More than $\frac{1}{2}$
ⓑ $\frac{1}{3}$
ⓒ Less than $\frac{1}{6}$
ⓓ $\frac{1}{4}$

3 The least amount of money is spent on _____.
ⓐ household bills
ⓑ clothing
ⓒ transportation
ⓓ entertainment

4 What part of the family's money is spent on clothing each month?
ⓐ 3%
ⓑ 6%
ⓒ 10%
ⓓ 22%

5 When Dad takes the bus to work each day, that cost is part of what category?
ⓐ transportation
ⓑ household bills
ⓒ clothing
ⓓ entertainment

6 Which cost is probably higher in winter than in summer?
ⓐ rent
ⓑ transportation
ⓒ household bills
ⓓ entertainment

Name _____ Date _____

Population Growth

The line graph below shows the number of people living in Newtown between 1900 and 2000. Use the graph to answer the questions.

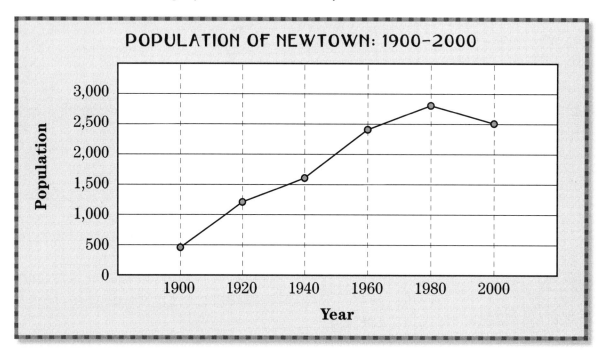

POPULATION OF NEWTOWN: 1900–2000

1 What was the population of Newtown in 1920?_____

2 How much did the population increase from 1920 to 1940?

_____

3 What was the population in 1960? _____

4 In which 20-year period did the size of the population change the most?

_____

5 Describe the general changes in Newtown's population from 1900 to 2000.

_____

_____

6 If this trend continues, what will the population of Newtown be in 2020?

_____

Name _____ Date _____

A Trip Through Time

The timeline below shows when different ways of telling time were invented. Use the timeline to answer the questions.

TIME MACHINE TIMELINE

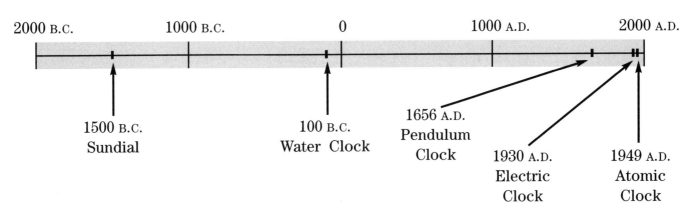

1 When was the sundial invented?
- (a) 1500 B.C.
- (b) 100 B.C.
- (c) 1656 A.D.
- (d) 1930 A.D.

2 Which type of clock was invented first?
- (a) atomic
- (b) pendulum
- (c) water
- (d) electric

3 What type of clock was invented in 1930?
- (a) pendulum
- (b) sundial
- (c) water
- (d) electric

4 This timeline covers about how many years?
- (a) 2000
- (b) 3000
- (c) 4000
- (d) 5000

5 For hundreds of years, people had to wind their clocks every day. When do you think winding became unnecessary? Explain why.

_____

_____

Name _____ Date _____

Mimi's Sunny Vacation

Mimi made a table to show when the sun rose and set each Saturday during her summer vacation. Use the table to answer the questions below.

SUNRISE AND SUNSET ON SUMMER SATURDAYS					
Date	Sunrise	Sunset	Date	Sunrise	Sunset
June 23	5:08 AM	8:25 PM	July 28	5:33 AM	8:08 PM
June 30	5:11 AM	8:25 PM	August 4	5:40 AM	8:00 PM
July 7	5:14 AM	8:23 PM	August 11	5:47 AM	7:51 PM
July 14	5:20 AM	8:20 PM	August 18	5:55 AM	7:41 PM
July 21	5:26 AM	8:15 PM	August 25	6:02 AM	7:30 PM

1 What time did the sun rise on July 21?

_____

2 On which date did the sun set at exactly 8:00 PM?

_____

3 Which Saturday had the earliest sunrise?

_____

4 How much earlier did the sun set on August 18 than on August 11?

_____

5 Which Saturday had exactly 15 hours between sunrise and sunset?

_____

6 How do the times of sunrise and sunset change from June 23 to the end of August?

_____

Name _____ Date _____

Weather Reporting

Fourth-grade students involved in a nation-wide project recorded the weather conditions each day for a week. Use the table to answer the questions below.

WEATHER DATA: SEPTEMBER 24–30					
Day	High Temperature	Low Temperature	Wind Speed (knots)	Precipitation	Conditions
Sunday	68°F	42°F	0–5	0	Sunny
Monday	69°F	44°F	0–5	0	Sunny
Tuesday	72°F	43°F	5–10	0	Cloudy
Wednesday	70°F	38°F	10–15	0	Partly Cloudy
Thursday	64°F	36°F	25–30	1.2 inches	Rainy
Friday	52°F	30°F	20–25	0.3 inches	Rainy
Saturday	52°F	32°F	10–15	0	Partly Cloudy

1 What were the high and low temperatures on Sunday?

_____

2 Which day was warmest? _____

3 On which days did the temperature go as low as the freezing point of 32°F?

_____

4 What were the weather conditions on Wednesday?

_____

5 In all, how much rain fell during the week? _____

6 Write one or two sentences describing how the weather changed from Sunday to Saturday.

_____

_____

Name _____ Date _____

Dining with Dinosaurs

This "Dino" chart provides specific information about different kinds of dinosaurs. Use the chart to choose the best answer to each question below.

DINOSAUR FACTS

Name	What It Means	Size	Weight	Food
Ankylosaurus	Crooked lizard	25 feet	3 tons	plants
Baryonyx	Heavy claw	30 feet	3,300 pounds	fish
Eoraptor	Dawn thief	3 feet	11–16 pounds	meat, insects
Maiasaura	Good mother lizard	30 feet	3 tons	plants
Plateosaurus	Broad lizard	20–26 feet	2,000–4,000 lb.	plants
Seismosaurus	Earthquake lizard	120–150 feet	40 tons	plants
Spinosaurus	Spined lizard	40 feet	4 tons	fish
Velociraptor	Fast thief	6 feet	30 pounds	meat

1 How much did the dinosaur called *Maiasaura* weigh?
- (a) 30 pounds
- (b) 3 tons
- (c) 4 tons
- (d) 40 tons

2 Which dinosaur's name means "broad lizard?"
- (a) *Ankylosaurus*
- (b) *Eoraptor*
- (c) *Plateosaurus*
- (d) *Spinosaurus*

3 How many feet long was the dinosaur called *Velociraptor*?
- (a) 3 feet
- (b) 6 feet
- (c) 25 feet
- (d) 30 feet

4 Which of these dinosaurs ate fish?
- (a) *Ankylosaurus*
- (b) *Maiasaura*
- (c) *Velociraptor*
- (d) *Spinosaurus*

5 Which is the largest, heaviest dinosaur listed in the chart?
- (a) *Seismosaurus*
- (b) *Plateosaurus*
- (c) *Eoraptor*
- (d) *Baryonyx*

40

Name _____   Date _____

How Hurricanes Get Their Names

When hurricanes form each year, the National Hurricane Center gives each one a name. The chart below shows some of the names for hurricanes in the Atlantic Ocean in the years 2002, 2003, and 2004. Use the chart to answer the questions.

HURRICANE NAMES: ATLANTIC OCEAN		
2002	2003	2004
Arthur	Ana	Alex
Bertha	Bill	Bonnie
Cristobal	Claudette	Charley
Dolly	Danny	Danielle
Edouard	Erika	Earl
Fay	Fabian	Frances
Gustav	Grace	Gaston
Hanna	Henri	Hermine
Isidore	Isabel	Ivan
Josephine	Juan	Jeanne
Kyle	Kate	Karl

1 What name will be given to the first hurricane in 2003?

_____

2 What name will be given to the fifth hurricane in 2004?

_____

3 What name came after Gustav in 2002?

_____

4 What name beginning with the letter "D" will be used in 2004?

_____

5 From this chart, what can you tell about the "rules" used in naming hurricanes? Explain your idea.

_____

_____

_____

_____

Name _____   Date _____

Speedy Animals

The bar graph below shows how fast some animals can run. Use the graph to answer the questions.

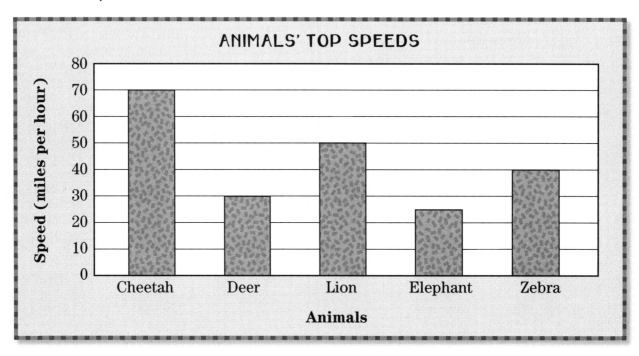

ANIMALS' TOP SPEEDS

1 How fast can a lion run? _____

2 How fast can an elephant run? _____

3 Which animal runs the fastest? _____

4 What is a zebra's top speed? _____

5 List all five animals in order from slowest to fastest.

_____

_____

_____

_____

_____

42

Name _____ Date _____

All About Energy

The circle graph below shows the sources of energy used in the United States today. Use the circle graph to choose the best answer to each question.

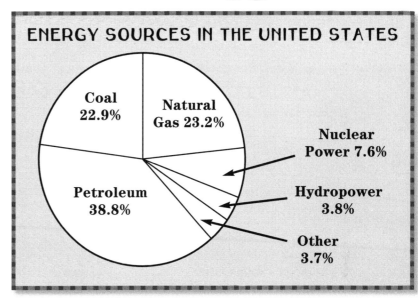

ENERGY SOURCES IN THE UNITED STATES

Coal 22.9% — Natural Gas 23.2% — Nuclear Power 7.6% — Hydropower 3.8% — Other 3.7% — Petroleum 38.8%

1 Which energy source provides about 8% of the power in the United States?
  (a) petroleum   (c) nuclear power
  (b) coal   (d) hydropower

2 What portion of the energy used in the United States comes from hydropower?
  (a) 38.8%   (c) 7.6%
  (b) 23.2%   (d) 3.8%

3 More than one third of the energy used in the United States comes from which source?
  (a) petroleum   (c) nuclear power
  (b) natural gas   (d) hydropower

4 About what percentage of energy used in the United States comes from fossil fuels (petroleum, natural gas, and coal)?
  (a) 65%   (c) 85%
  (b) 75%   (d) 95%

5 From this graph, you can conclude that the energy in the United States provided by solar power is _____.
  (a) less than 4%   (c) about 10%
  (b) about 4%   (d) more than 10%

Name _____ Date _____

Cleveland's Weather Update

The line graph below shows the average temperature each month in Cleveland, Ohio. Use the graph to answer the questions.

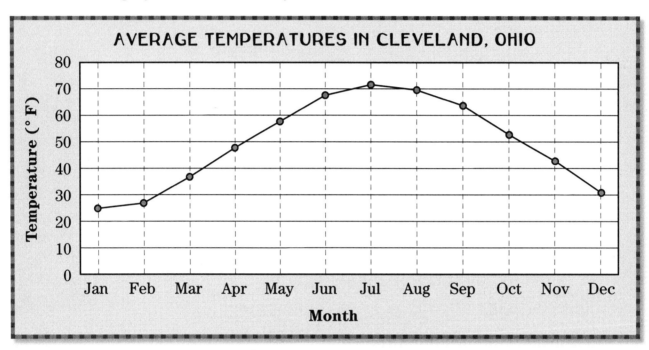

1 What is the average temperature in Cleveland in March? _____

2 What is the average temperature in Cleveland in September? _____

3 Which is the warmest month? _____

4 Which is the coldest month? _____

5 What is the difference in average temperature between the warmest month and the coldest? _____

6 Write one or two sentences that describe the changes in temperature during the year.

_____

_____

_____

Mathematics

TABLE: The Winning Team

(page 6)

1. c
2. b
3. d
4. a
5. b

TABLE: Measuring Up

(page 7)

1. 60 in.
2. 24 pounds
3. Teresita and Pablo
4. Size 5
5. The sizes get larger, or the numbers increase.

TALLY CHART: Tori's Sandwich Study

(page 8)

1. b
2. a
3. c
4. d

TALLY CHART: Pete's Chores

(page 9)

1. a
2. d
3. b
4. d

PICTOGRAPH: Drew's Newspaper Route

(page 10)

1. a
2. a
3. b
4. c

PICTOGRAPH: Cool Inventions

(page 11)

1. Computer
2. 30
3. Automobile and telephone
4. 20

BAR GRAPH: The Class Field Trip

(page 12)

1. a
2. c
3. b
4. h

BAR GRAPH: Hannah and Her Cousins

(page 13)

1. 2
2. Vermont
3. 1
4. 16

BAR GRAPH: Soccer Contest

(page 14)

1. b
2. d
3. b
4. c

BAR GRAPH: Scouts' Honors

(page 15)

1. 5
2. 3
3. Nature
4. 31
5. The Science badge is probably most difficult because it has been earned by the fewest scouts.

BAR GRAPH: Zack's Lazy Afternoon

(page 16)

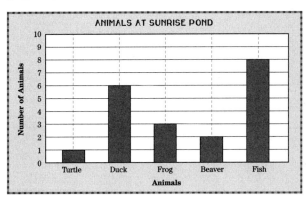

CIRCLE GRAPH: The Class Takes a Trip
(page 17)
1. Science museum
2. 5
3. Water park and amusement park
4. Amusement park
5. Example: The water park would get the fewest votes; the science museum would get a lot more votes.

CIRCLE GRAPH: Recycling Efforts
(page 18)
1. d
2. a
3. d
4. b
5. c

LINE GRAPH: Best-Selling Books
(page 19)
1. 21
2. Thursday
3. 8
4. 29
5. About 13 books

LINE GRAPH: Compare the Squares
(page 20)
1. 16 in.
2. 5 in.
3. 20 sq. in.
4. 3.5 in.
5. Example: The area of a square increases rapidly as the sides of the square become longer.

Reading/Language Arts

CHART: Adorable Animals
(page 21)
1. c
2. a
3. d
4. c
5. a

CHART: Joel's Trip Planner
(page 22)
1. Hiking, camping
2. 4
3. Lilac Lake and Mead Canyon
4. Mead Canyon
5. Underwood Park

CHART: Ordering Dinner
(page 23)
1. a
2. c
3. b
4. c

CHART: The Bookworm Club
(page 24)
1. *Amy Grows Up*
2. $2.95
3. 5
4. *Dinosaur Dig*, $4.50

TABLE: Niko's Aquarium
(page 25)
1. b
2. a
3. d
4. d

TABLE: Card Sharks
(page 26)
1. c
2. a
3. b
4. d

Social Studies

TABLE: School Birthdays (page 27)
1. 2
2. July
3. 5
4. Spring
5. April

TABLE: Presidential Studies

(page 28)

1. c
2. b
3. d
4. c
5. a

CHART: Beautiful Bridges

(page 29)

1. Verrazano-Narrows
2. Mackinac Straits, Michigan
3. California, 1937
4. 3,500 feet
5. Delaware Memorial and Tacoma Narrows

CHART: The Wild Wild West

(page 30)

1. Olympia
2. 1890
3. Oregon
4. Lark Bunting
5. Oregon
6. Sagebrush
7. Idaho and Nevada both have the mountain bluebird.

CHART: The Story of Paper

(page 31)

1. Logs are chipped into small pieces.
2. Wood pulp is cleaned and beaten into slush.
3. Step 4, Screen
4. Heat is used to cook the wood chips and to dry the web.

PICTOGRAPH: Building Houses

(page 32)

1. 60 houses
2. Franklin County
3. Langham County
4. 25 houses
5. The answer should show $4\frac{1}{5}$ house symbols.

BAR GRAPH: How Does Susan's Garden Grow?

(page 33)

1. c
2. d
3. b
4. c
5. b

BAR GRAPH: Alex the Sports Reporter

(page 34)

Examples of Correct Responses:

1.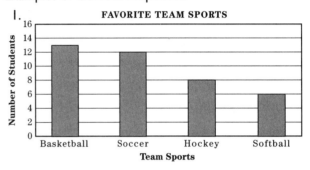

2.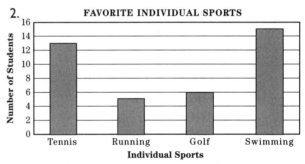

CIRCLE GRAPH: Mindy Minds the Money

(page 35)

1. b
2. d
3. d
4. b
5. a
6. c

LINE GRAPH: Population Growth

(page 36)

1. About 1200
2. About 400
3. About 2400
4. 1940–1960
5. Example: The population grew steadily from 1900 to 1980, and then it began to decline.
6. Probably between 2,000 and 2,200

TIMELINE: A Trip Through Time
(page 37)
1. a
2. c
3. d
4. c
5. Example: Winding became unnecessary in 1930 when electric clocks were invented.

Science

TABLE: Mimi's Sunny Vacation
(page 38)
1. 5:26 AM
2. August 4
3. June 23
4. 10 minutes
5. July 14
6. The sun rises later each day and sets earlier.

TABLE: Weather Reporting
(page 39)
1. 68°F, 42°F
2. Tuesday
3. Friday and Saturday
4. Partly cloudy
5. 1.5 inches
6. Example: It was warm until Wednesday, and then it got cooler each day. It got cloudy and rainy on Thursday and Friday.

CHART: Dining with Dinosaurs
(page 40)
1. b
2. c
3. b
4. d
5. a

CHART: How Hurricanes Get Their Names
(page 41)
1. Ana
2. Earl
3. Hanna
4. Danielle
5. Example: In each year, names alternate between male and female. In even-numbered years, the first name is male. In odd-numbered years, the first name is female.

BAR GRAPH: Speedy Animals
(page 42)
1. 50 mph
2. 25 mph
3. Cheetah
4. 40 mph
5. Elephant, deer, zebra, lion, cheetah

CIRCLE GRAPH: All About Energy
(page 43)
1. c
2. d
3. a
4. c
5. a

LINE GRAPH: Cleveland's Weather Update
(page 44)
1. 37°F
2. 64°F
3. July
4. January
5. 47°F
6. Example: The average temperature rises steadily each month from January through July, and then it drops steadily from July through December.